AF327182

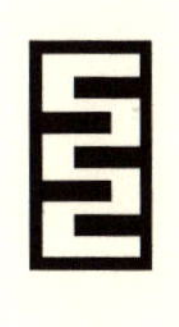

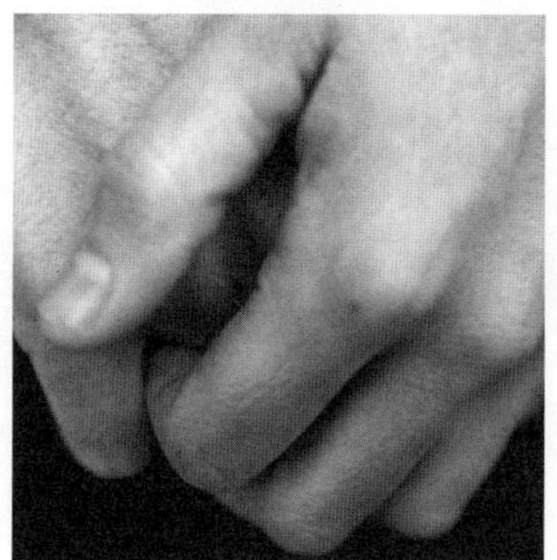

PAM REHM

Gone to Earth

FLOOD EDITIONS

Chicago 2001

FLOOD EDITIONS P.O. Box 3865, Chicago, Illinois 60654-0865
This edition first published in paperback by Flood Editions
FIRST PAPERBACK EDITION
Copyright © 2001 by Pam Rehm
All rights reserved

Some of these poems previously appeared in *apex of the M, Chicago Review, LVNG, Talisman, & Anthology of New (American) Poetry*

Cover by Jeff Marlin
Frontispiece of the author's hands by Cindy Rehm

ISBN 0-9710059-1-5

Printed in the United States of America on acid-free paper

CONTENTS

There are some things that it is necessary
to believe; doubt of them means despair.

MARY WEBB, *Gone to Earth*

A roof is no guarantee
that you'll sleep

The unease of premises
pins together the curtains
at night

Waiting for a clearness
of purpose

Eating 3 meals a day
we go to bed hungry

Privacy is not a remedy

We've become separated
by "efficiencies"
Nobody can do anything with

A kind of machine person
Floundering in the dark

It's hard to believe
5 sparrows were sold for this

Of Single Intent

Whenever you're absent
I make a likeness of you

In the soil or the river
Something innocent and free

Where I blaze my own trail
Your heart is a frontier

To you,
I was persuaded approach

First "darkly"
but then "face to face"

Shepherded

Out of the thicket
Hand in hand

An awakening kiss
Spoken under the rose

We came to this beginning
at the point of contact

An almost hypnotic effect

A figment becomes fact

The bird or boy's face

Held by home
the dice are thrown

The letters in the name
rearranged

To see the world within
the word begin

The word is my word

The world is my surmise

An ecstasy first yielding
to the eyes
when I awake without alarm

To be all curiosity

Naturally desiring
a day with you
That strays into night

There is your presence
A trial of the individual

There is your absence
An individual trial

Your words beat against
days of desire

My heart was once more exalted

The fault is to only gain
what is coveted
in confusion and harm

Thus, I have become as a beast

I am a worm
that I may learn what earth is

But to find its intimacy
is a rarity

A lost acre

Acres and acres of loss

Calling out a first name

My scribe
I have tried to beckon expression

Groping for your recognition

I listen and listen

੬ह

The night purloined

Going from one another
in the deviation of a dream

Despite everything

Robbed by the impetuousness
of love

7

Free to rest without ambivalence
Intention is difficult to express

I want to follow your tracks
to the exact rhythm

To exchange positions
You become Instinct, and I, Protection

Burning with life

I dream of no heaven
except one on the hillsides

Ascending

Where the fire is
in your eyes

Unceasingly beheld
by mine

An Empty Account

The simplest relationships happen without
any expectation, this is what I believe

The infatuation in a girl's cheeks

The eyes of a man when he looks on

My spouse, I am poor

I'm a paper situation

Year by year
year after year

There have been a string of bad years

I sit at a large table

Words don't unravel overnight

The kingdom of money
and the kingdom of memory

The necessity to bend one's head forward

Nothing but a blind prompting

A woman turned to Him, you know
His mouth a towel into which

His resigning

His panic stricken resignation

was withdrawn

This overwhelming lamentation

The things that are never confided

A child walking and running

He takes hold of my hand
fascinated by the squirrel

Something deeper than "use"

I could love home in a deep sense

The Concept of Dread

1

Your business in this world
Your nakedness and terror

Your sanctity remains
the crucial battle

Dearly beyond
we are scattered here today

amongst commodities

This town isn't big enough
for trust

An internal theatre

the metaphors for
(secret)

Within oneself a beggar

No need for another
authority

2

A metamorphosis
is latent in me, in this city

"Everything leads to one point"

I confuse myself
with your coming

Silently cursing
these buildings

Restless
after an exhausting walk

You are precisely
what I struggle against

3

Thoughts that you are not equal
to writing

Thoughts that you are not able
to conquer

Pleading like Gloucester

in the middle of the middle
"engulfed"

an irreparable loss

"eaten away by time"

4

There's tension in the question
of what salvation saves

To continue to be guilty

To be continually tempted

The drama
forever in play

Everyday you occur
the core
Confrontation

5

Anguish
a singular closure

I only feel the chaos

The insomnia of my heart

Always there's a price
to pay, offer

Out into a darker night

The insanity of love

Could no longer see anything
In the suspicion of desire

Immediately lost and no longer

6

There's no rest
as far as I know

You're pressed under
an unpredictable pillow

"only the immensity is known"

You turn to it for affection

I turn to it to lose you

I'm guilty

"Cover my face with ashes"

"We Realize a Guilt ..."

We realize a guilt
in its aftermath
We can't go out
in
The staying power
A torment keeps
Restricted to the minds
meetings or feelings finds
What we think is imminent
is already far behind
Missed in the missing
You have lost me
The cost a debt
I grow in

Serving Two Masters

1

Perpetrator,
Where do you come from?

Hidden in spite

Where did you come from
when you came out of me?

Oh me, of little
mercy

All ploys are empty
Prudency

My mind a parasite

How deep is a hole
my soul wants to know

Will love always defy
description?

2

I feel deaf
inside of possessions

I'm not the world
but its vanity
has a hold on me

Today, I wasn't wearing clothes
I liked

This image I apprehend
through a stream of tears

One dance is enough
to corrupt

Fidelity

To forget, accordingly

Then be overcome with regret

3

When you elude pursuit
I am free

to reason

Thus, become filled
with worrying

A broken temper

In despondence

Am I at home
or letting go

When I picture myself alive
I do not know what will come
out of me

Tomorrow

I try to change
before falling asleep

4

In spite of its preference
Solitude
merely maintains a childish "take"

So where shall we go
and to whom

When I stop belonging
to my room

You stop belonging *to* me

In this way I will submit myself

No love should be kept
Precious

The Humiliation of the Valley

1

The compass of the moment
reveals an angle of suspense
Doubtful hope or bliss to come
are the only presentiments
pressed heavy in the air
of circumspect

Scarcely do we venture
to admit patience
without prospect
but depict ourselves under
an unspeakable oppression
Cold and peculiar
Independent and somewhat suspicious

Days are passed enacted
And there is no end
come to, to note them

2

Nowhere a center and everywhere
a periphery

Until you're wounded in a single spot
Permanently
no impression is made

When conscience is mortalized
you submit to its governance
The only saving grace
is to release the adder
feeding in the breast

3

Never betray what is received
An undying elemental stream

The imagination forges
an endless penetration
an unquestionable possession
that escapes you through the air
of the centuries

Beguiling the tedium of the way
like an instrument blown
out of scale

What name is on the lips
and in my flesh?
You leave yourself again and again
The tone is infinite
Presence the forever unanswered question

4

Ambivalence is seldom a stimulus
It retains a sentiment of protection

Acquainted with few acquaintances
you beg of yourself amusement
In a paroxysm of dialects
To evince a base spirit
To discern a voice within you

What is this leading to?

To recipient, known—
You must follow
an evolution out of
dead notions
Feed on nutrients not notoriety
nonetheless piety
For your only possession
is being possessed

Furthermore, there is trial
in commitment
You'd be witless without it
and much too deliberate

A Trivial Pursuit

1

A wonder the scene is
Psyche

Not knowing knowing
to see

Becoming lovers
before there were arrows

There was an Eros
prior to awakening

Thus, crucified into affection
my Eros is curious
in the dark

Wrought with primal force,
the source of trembling

The wound, the mother-lode
of all figure and fable

The children are hidden
from the table

We are all changelings
evoking ourselves

2

Desire for the possession of happiness

Apprehension of an all-embracing
Attraction

Half-way between interaction
Images of images

Oh my right hand
What am I to do

Let the whole house crash
from mood to mood?

Passion moves
lacking in foresight
with a joy of its own

I heard a person saying
Hide this from me

But where can we hide
to escape life's chorus?

3

One cannot avoid impressions
The pressure suggesting a system
of surrender

to attachment or self-confession

A superstitious regard for salvation
and the soul

Each year forever
a fury

To have ten-thousand words
Stained

You are bound to lose your tongue

Hiding from yourself
the things you fear
will mean something

4

Shadows of images
Images in reflection

Implied is the memory,
all embracing

Possessed by guilt
and its preservation

My Eros is curious
for explanation

The heart a fire

Trembling in the dark

A figure moves
in and out of

Where Oh Where
Has My Little God Gone

FOR ELIZABETH WILLIS

By what are you thwarted?
A pioneer is said to have
                the Clouds
and to escape the evils of life
holds up Hephaestus
in the face of civilization

What good are miracles
What is a fact

There are stories
in order to make
heaven
unlike the other fragments
that have come down to us

Not to speak is not not-being
For it is impossible to speak
about being divided by something

Nothing is altogether self-ruled

Economic life
will run down blind alleys
a specter

"Eternity's curtain"
pulled by purse strings

Once apprehended
the coin becomes a relic
diminished by the number
of deaths in our time

The gibbering shades of the departed

It is absurd to speak
of the spirit presenting itself
to make us live again

The body is an echo
in the shadow-image of Pantheism

It is important to realize
that a demon is highly pristine

And that all things still perish
from praying well

The dichotomy
is an inseparable aspect

Nothing without recompense

In weakness and in absence
Interaction becomes anonymous

Practicing to speak and writing
to deceive dialogue

No one can hope to make virtue
a notion or policy
to promote the politician's career

Sorrow is the condition
of an unpleasant outlook

So the moral to be drawn
is not to deny you want to travel

We all struggle with the problem
"Of what is the world ultimately
composed?"

Rationality changes with the season
Passion so to darken reason

Guesswork and imitation
There are no premises

"appearing to" must mean "becoming for"
No longer forced into form

Fate loves to step twice
into reality

Poised in one place
Sympathy unites me with other things

Lying awake in bed
I dream of interpreting the wakened state

Into one day and out of another
now means the Abyss itself

It is common sense
to become a tenant of idealism

Trying to weld the name of a god to anyone
is preferable

There are so many things
to touch and to hold
but not own

There is indeed
no real evidence
that words would appear naturally

in other words
in other words

The beginning of language
meant to establish the end
of speculative thought

Thus, transcendentalism
is not as enlightening as a fairy-tale

For there are so many histories
dealing with a certain lifting
of the eyebrows

The lexicon says it stands for
"this bondage I am"

Yet the woods are more distressing

Turning turns manifestly solitary
The senses turn mendicant

Survival is the realist master

So where are you within me
Where am I without you

Glimpses of a longing unrequited

What does pleasure resemble

I cannot describe for I am afraid
against the sunset
figuring like a child
how the whole of light disappears,
          strangely
among the pebbles, sundered down

Into one night and out of another

To be self-controlled
does not consist in having morals

The habit of impulse
comes upon desirability

What woman is safe

As if among the bitter-sweet poisons
Hell needed to tell something
pounding the word it stood for

I regard it as weak, I think
at times intolerable to play out
the inexorable will of belief

I cannot follow any form
of intending
other than a reservation
to cast my gaze yonder

So many ways to the future

Grass a portion of everything

School children mingling
Two dogs follow

The geese overhead
Led without tracks

We move hither now thither
towards something

Only to be drowned crossing the river

November Testament

Always a coward
I play the bully

Then beg you
to forgive me

I know it is absurd

When the night cometh
in the silence before dawn

But how shall I look for you,
my soul
I cannot tell time

to stop
I have lost so much
by refusal

A strange reciprocity
once leveled us

Now I can't explain

The empty window
within sight

Cut short of light
the cold has entered

I toss the leaves
and go back in

᠅

Do you know this fugue
It keeps going around
in my head

Like persistent rage

I cannot escape
impelling it

Pray,
teach me a better craft
than dependence

᠅

In one drawer we save
From another we spend

It is one and the same

We are without relations
We have become partitions

We eat from a table
of exclusion

We hear noises
as if they were *meant* for us

We are already burying our children

※

The pauper is equally
our impoverished witnessing

A sign
of our ridiculous lives
on this bank of the river

"What depends on us"
is not "all" or "nothing"

If I nourish myself
If I am sufficient to myself

Who am I then,

Enough?

How often do we touch
our learning?

Paper money
and men's perceptions

What is a profit
and how will it redeem us?

Our hands remain useless

Private

Manipulated
has a man in it

A human centeredness
Where nothing else can enter
Let alone survive

Let Me Enter

If I stopped
trying to find you

Would I lose
my mind

Homesick
When I walk out

This road

No sound

Tangled thicket of the heart

The soul is little known
behind a mirror

Have I chosen this
Binding

Because the world persists
my devotion turns to bitterness

A witness and yet still standing

Is my own conviction imperative
or a false idol

like silence

An insufferable curtaining

A forlorn remoteness

After a night of hesitation
the snow has come

A slipping path

I can't decide what I need most

Revelations or rest

I just want to be stilled
by love

to such a depth
that I'm forgotten

Among the flowers

To die for what is not mine

Your meaning is upon me

Gone to Earth

Beyond innocence
the exhibition
of obedient faith
is precedent

Work on the limits

A limit of what can be thought
outlives ambivalence

You work yourself to death

To enlarge an abstract
madness

Never so divine
a will

One step further
and the bed is no longer
under you

and no letter

I'm out of humor

This is for the you
In my memory

A picture
you would be the better of

You have hidden yourself well,
in attention

Little else to occupy your heart

Small change

The birds spreading their wings
to which I am joined

ABOUT THE AUTHOR

Pam Rehm lives in New York City with her husband and two children. She is the author of four previous collections: *Pollux, Piecework, The Garment in Which No One Had Slept,* and *To Give It Up* (winner of the National Poetry Series for 1994).